THIS BOOK BELONGS TO

....

To Archie, my inspiration.
To Ric, for all you do for us.
To Dad, who I miss everyday.

Archiesaurus woke up and roared a loud yawn,
He was excited for today.
Later he was meeting his friends at the dino park,
To run, laugh and play.

YAAWWWWNNN

He chomped his cereal and gulped his juice,
Rushing, he got dressed as quickly as he could.
He wanted to get to the park and go on the swings,
Like all his friends would.

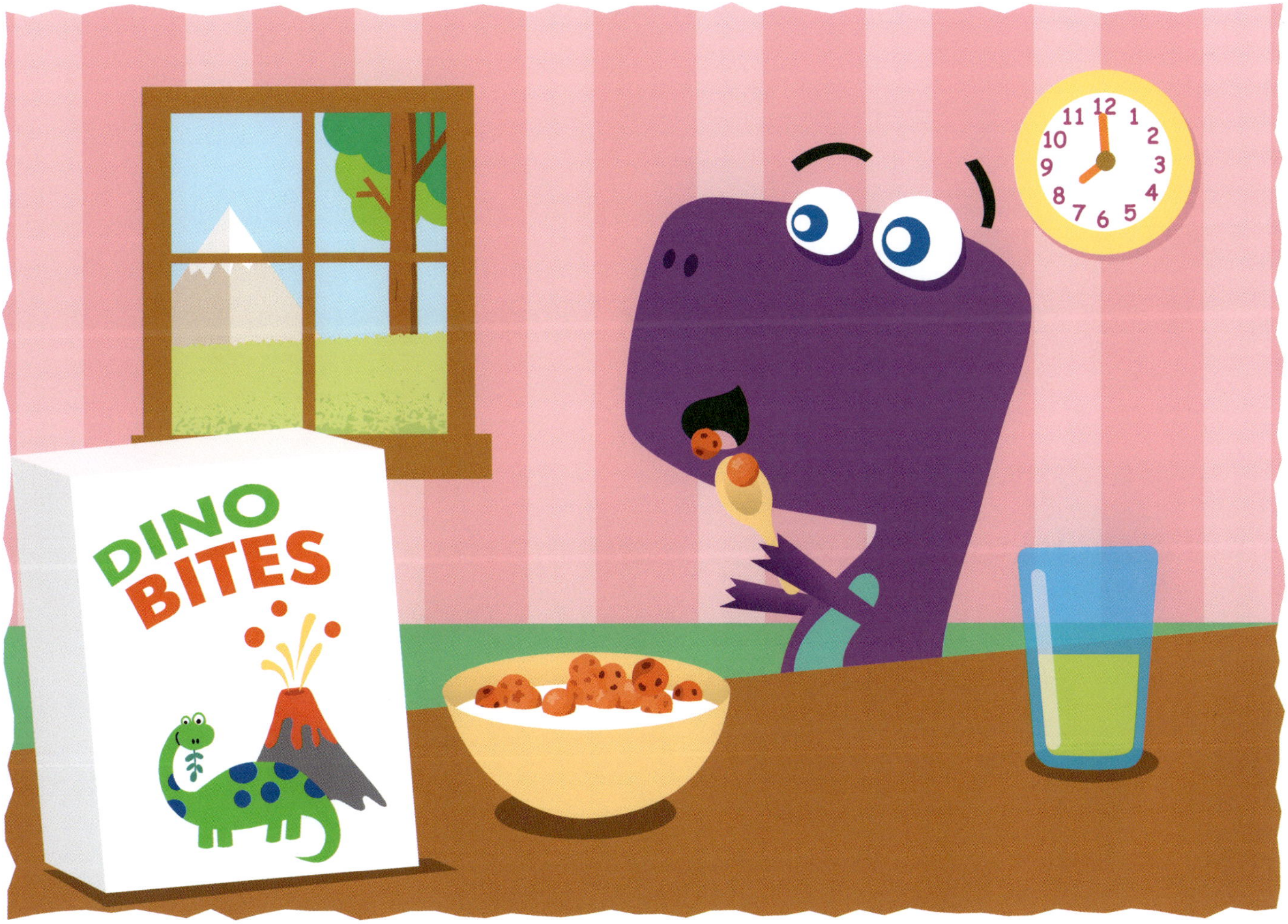
DINO
BITES

Archiesaurus roared

"I am off to the dino park Mummysaurus!"

As he sprinted out the door.

Mummysaurus roared

"Watch out for woolly mammoths on the road,

Or you will be squashed to the floor!".

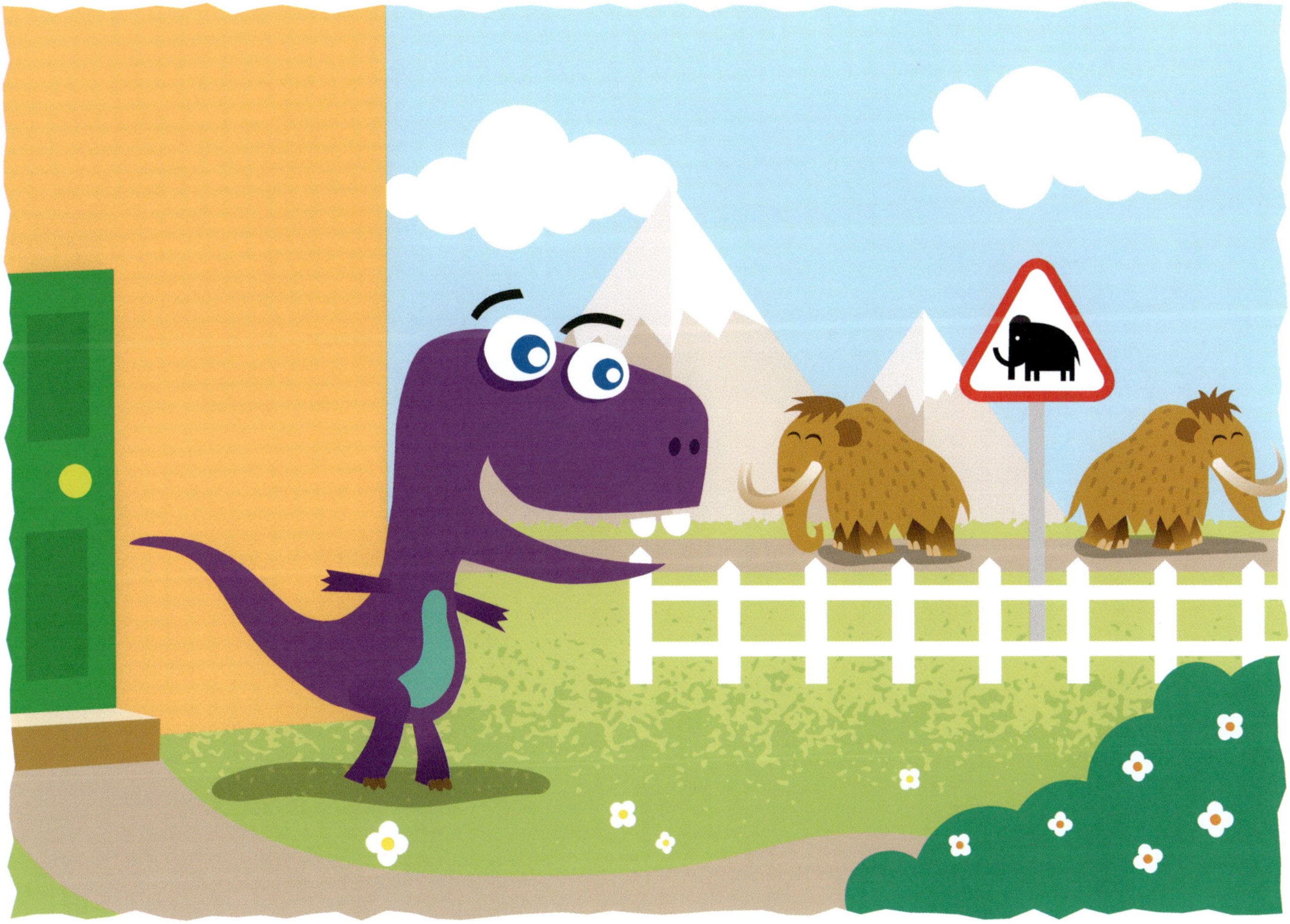

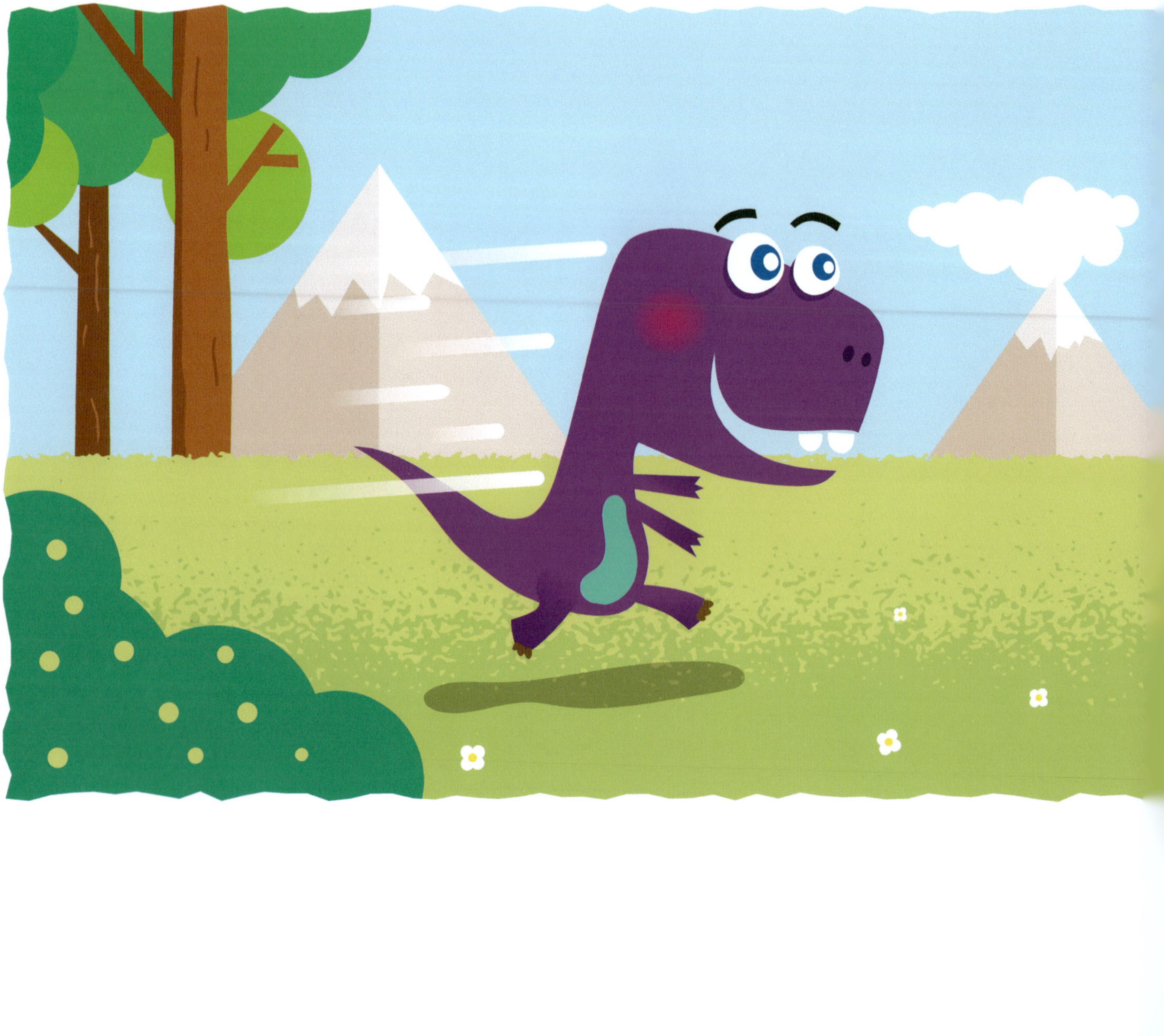

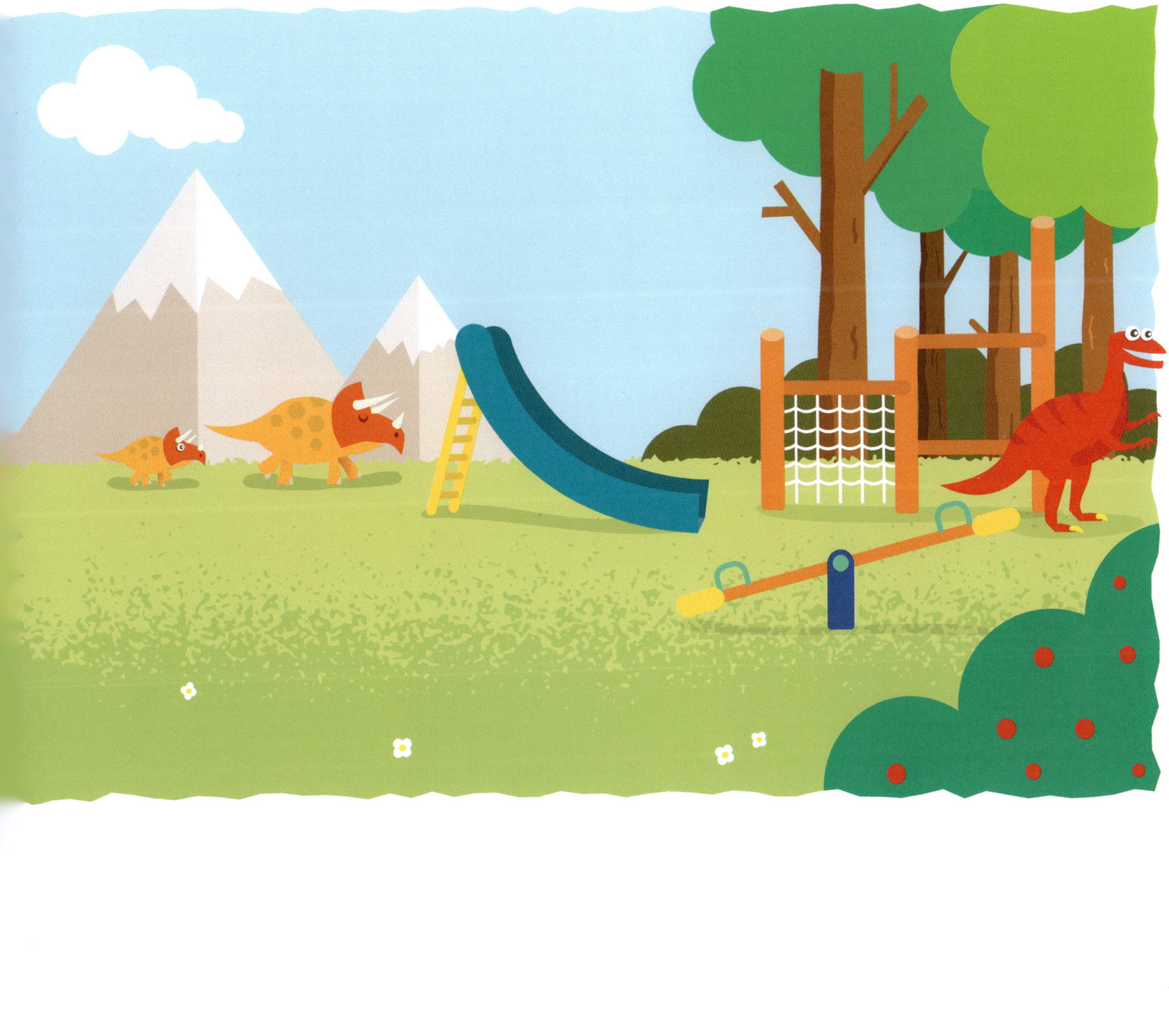

Theodontasurus was on the slide,

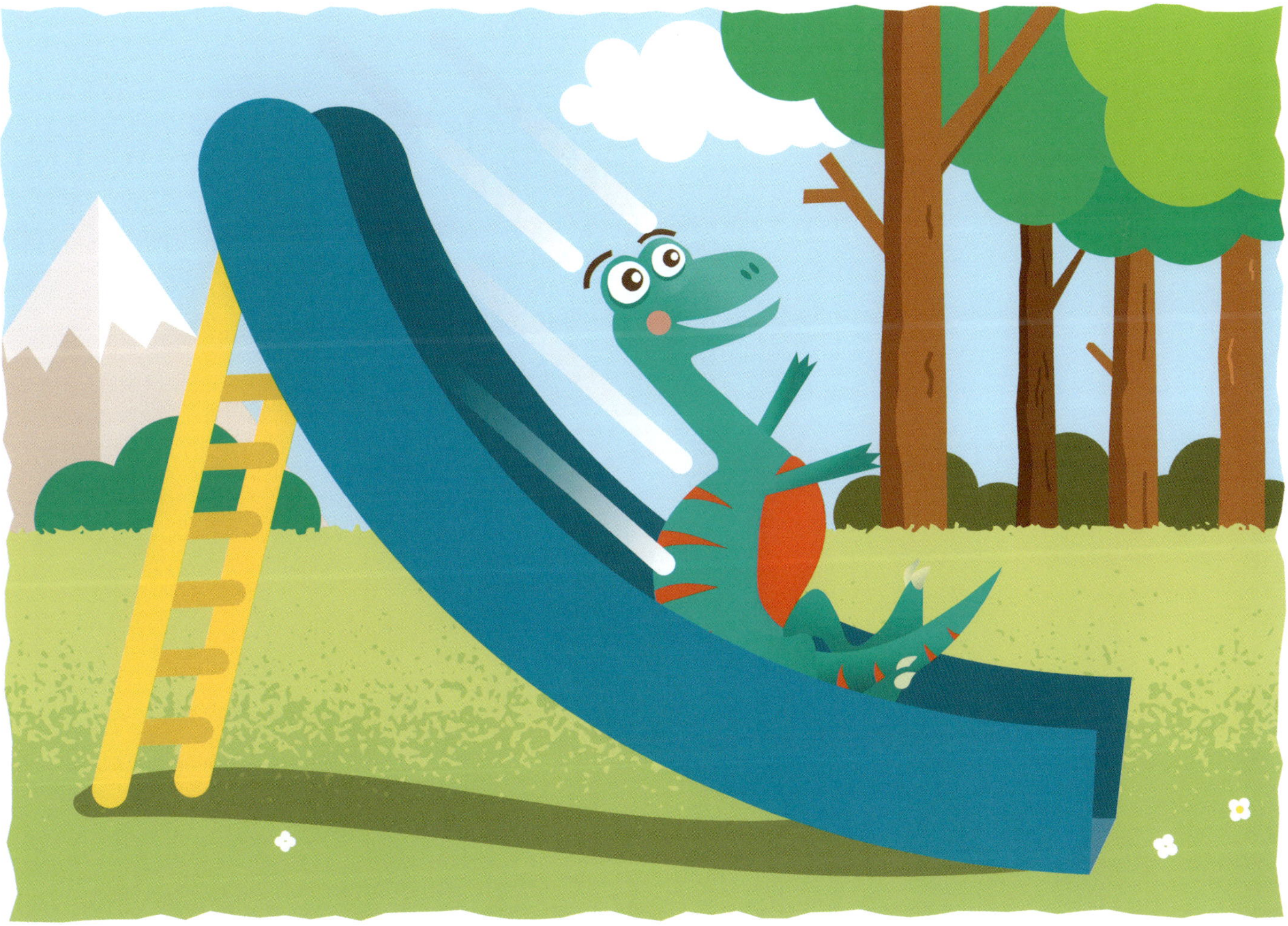

Steffosaurus was on the climbing frame.

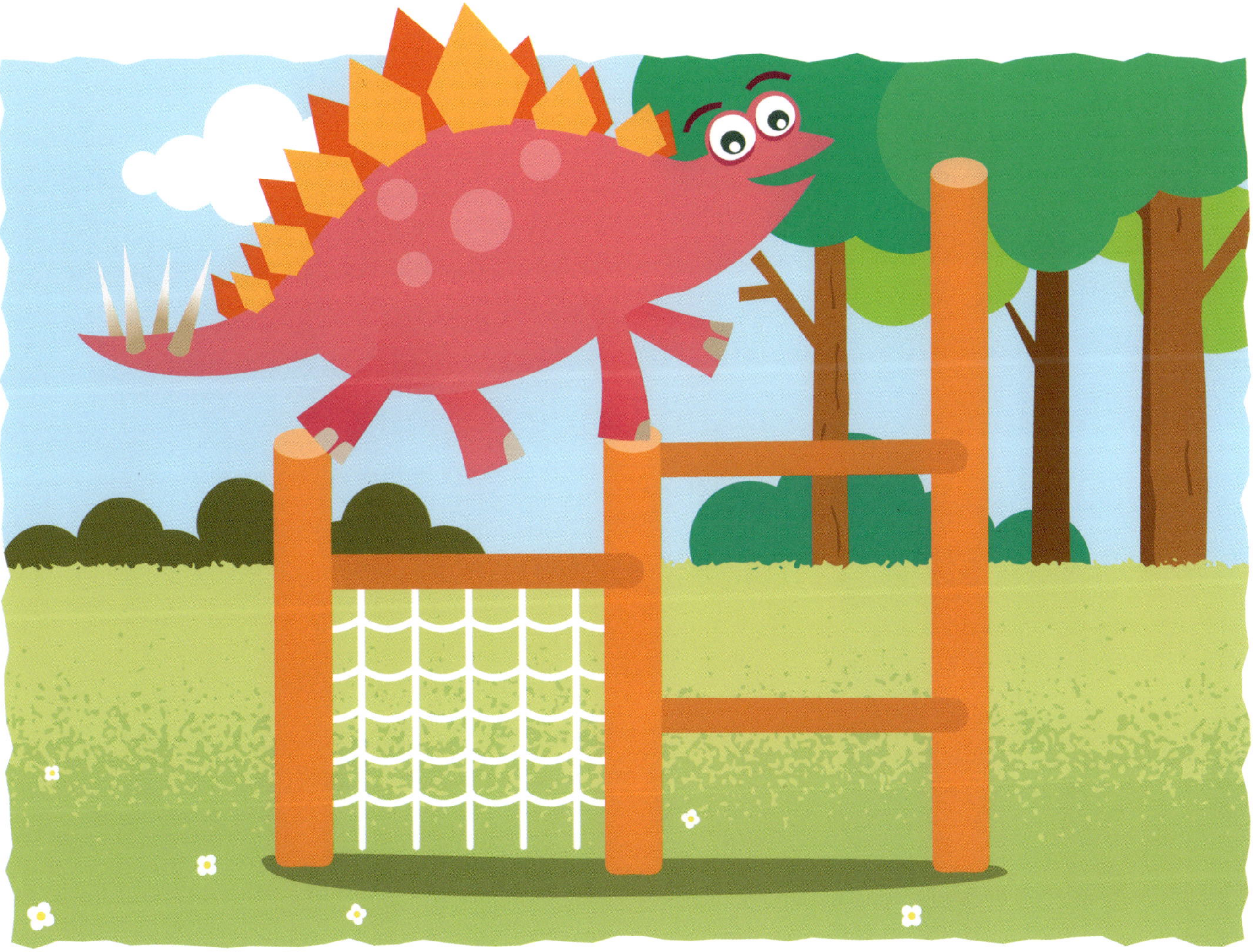

Archiesaurus was on the swings when, Teddydactyl screeched
"Do you all want to play a game?"

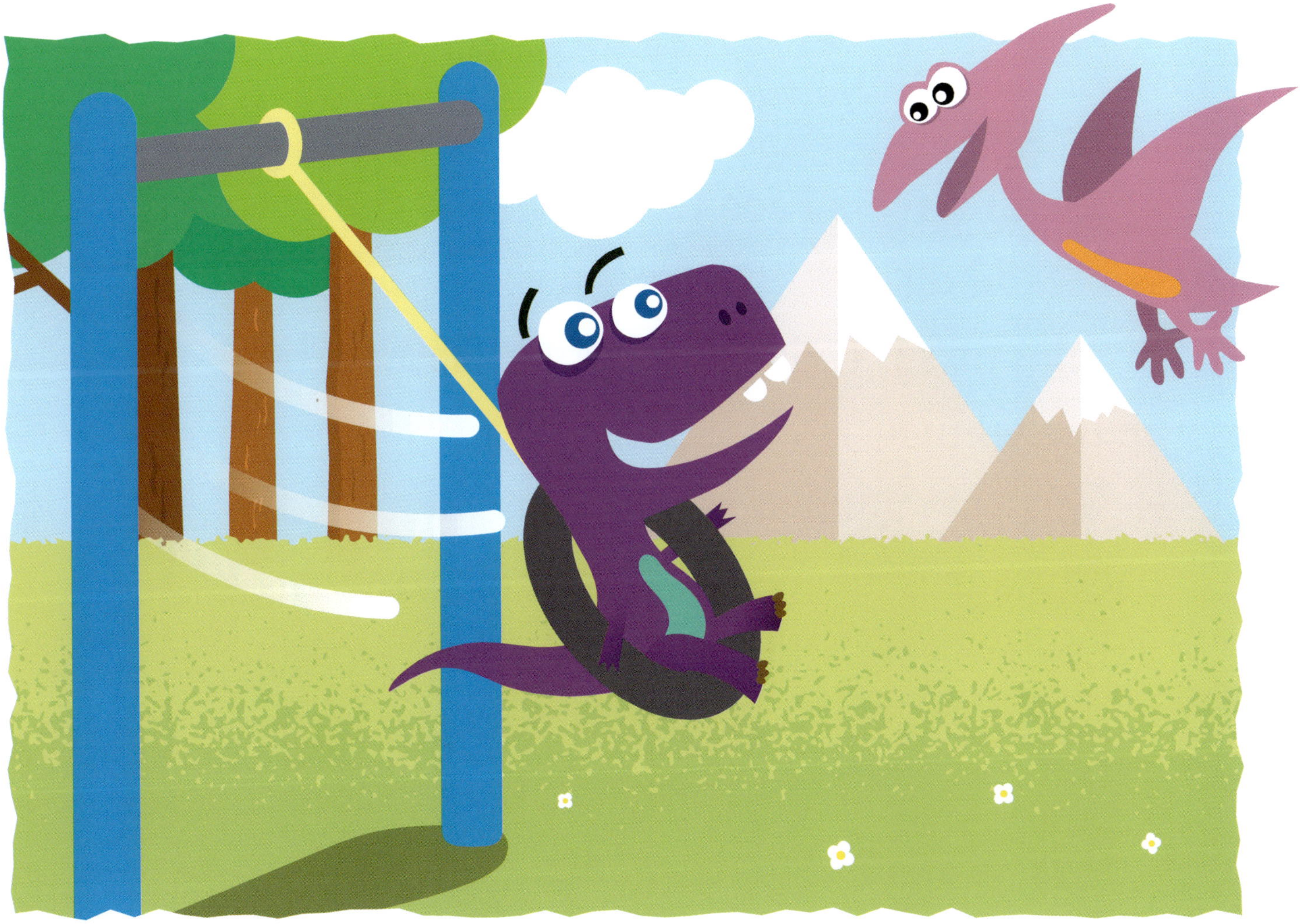

"We can have a race to see who is the fastest,"
said Teddydactyl

Archiesaursus thought he would definitely
be the winner.

He was very good at running fast,
Daddysaurus always said he would grow big and
strong if he ate all his dinner.

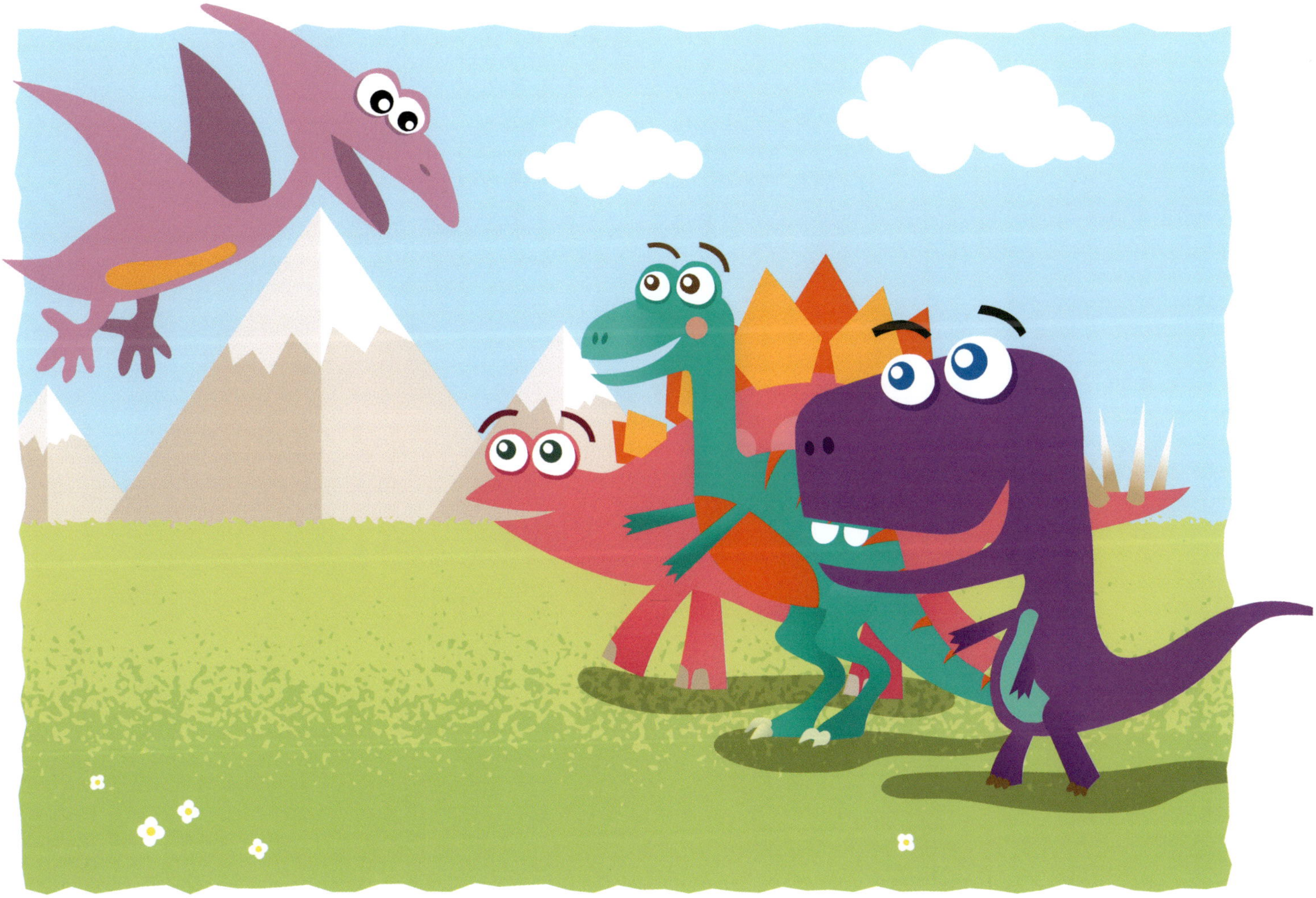

All the dinosaurs got in a line,
READY
        STEADY
                GO!

START

Archiesaurus began running very fast.
Steffosaurus was trying hard but with the heavy spikes on her tail,
Feared she would come last.

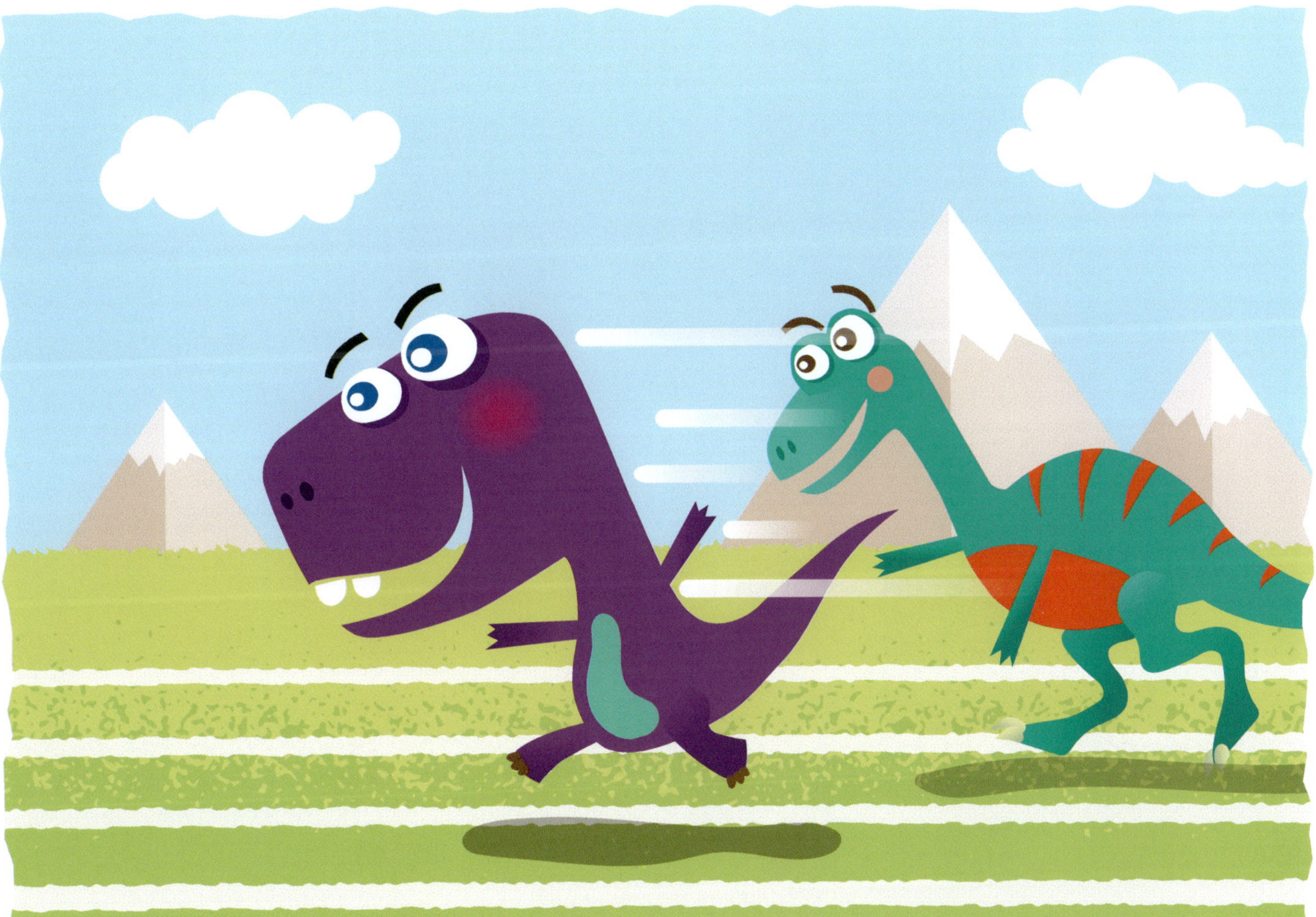

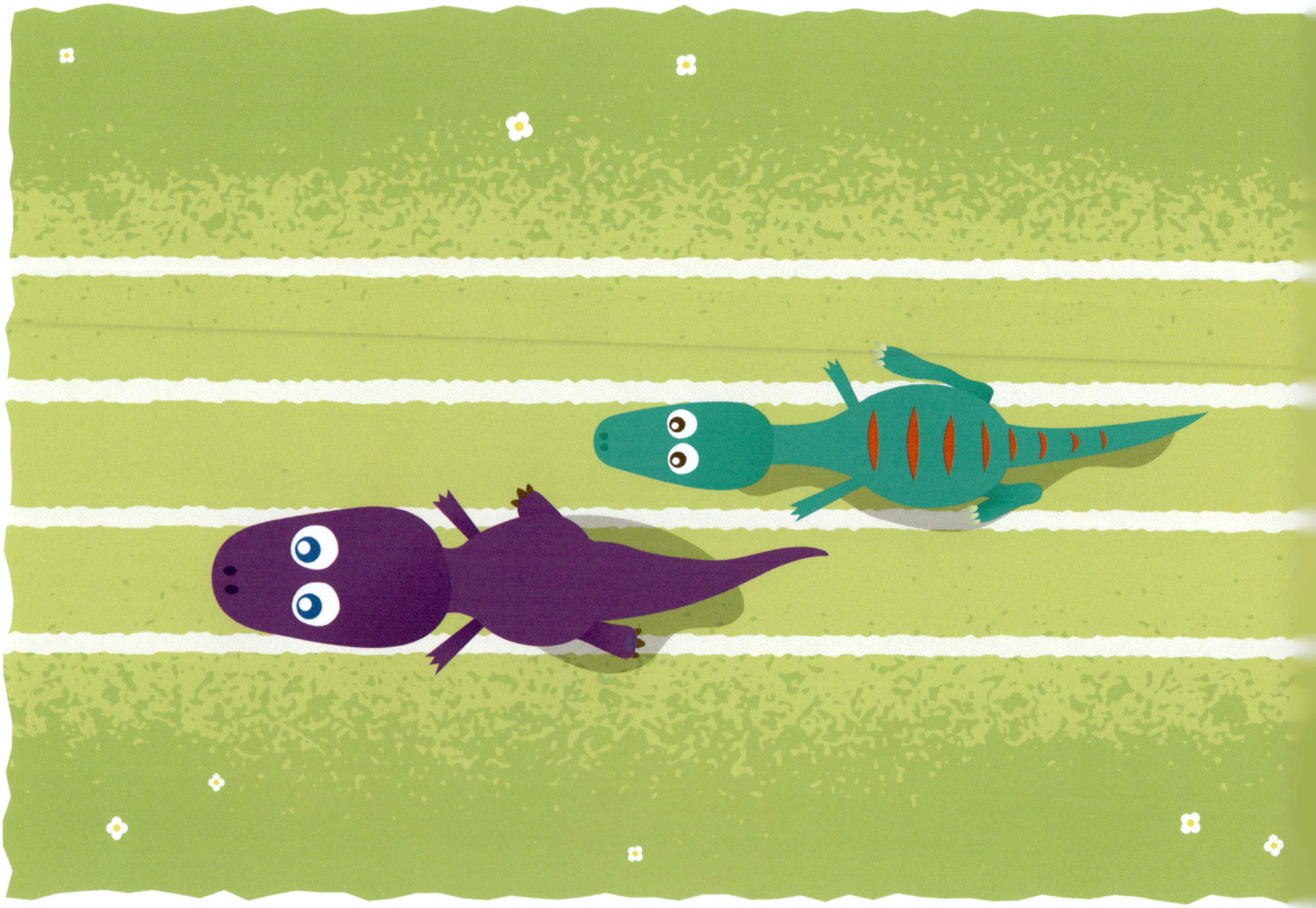

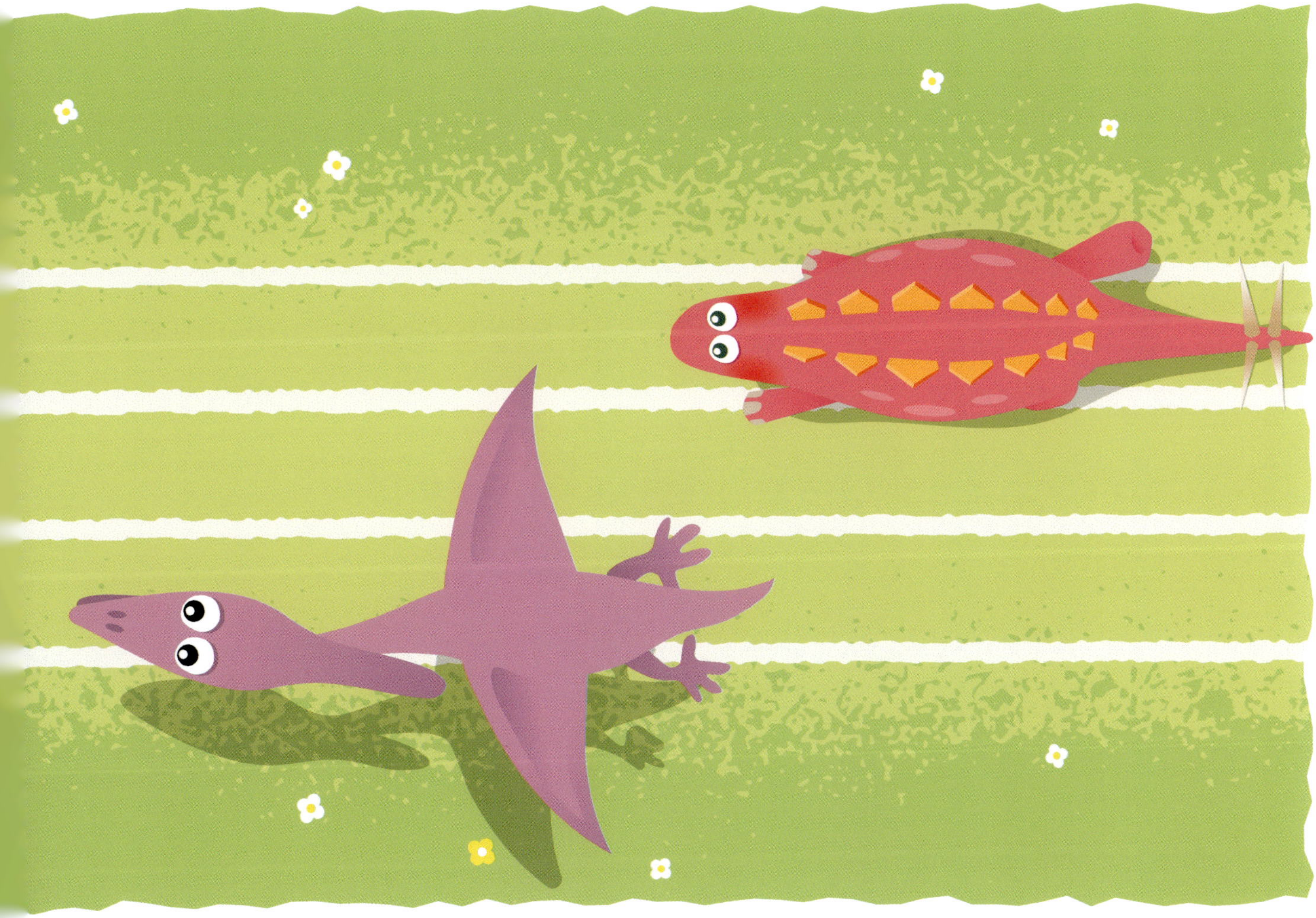

Archiesaurus turned and realised his friend was at the back,
He didn't want anyone to feel sad if they lost and started to frown.

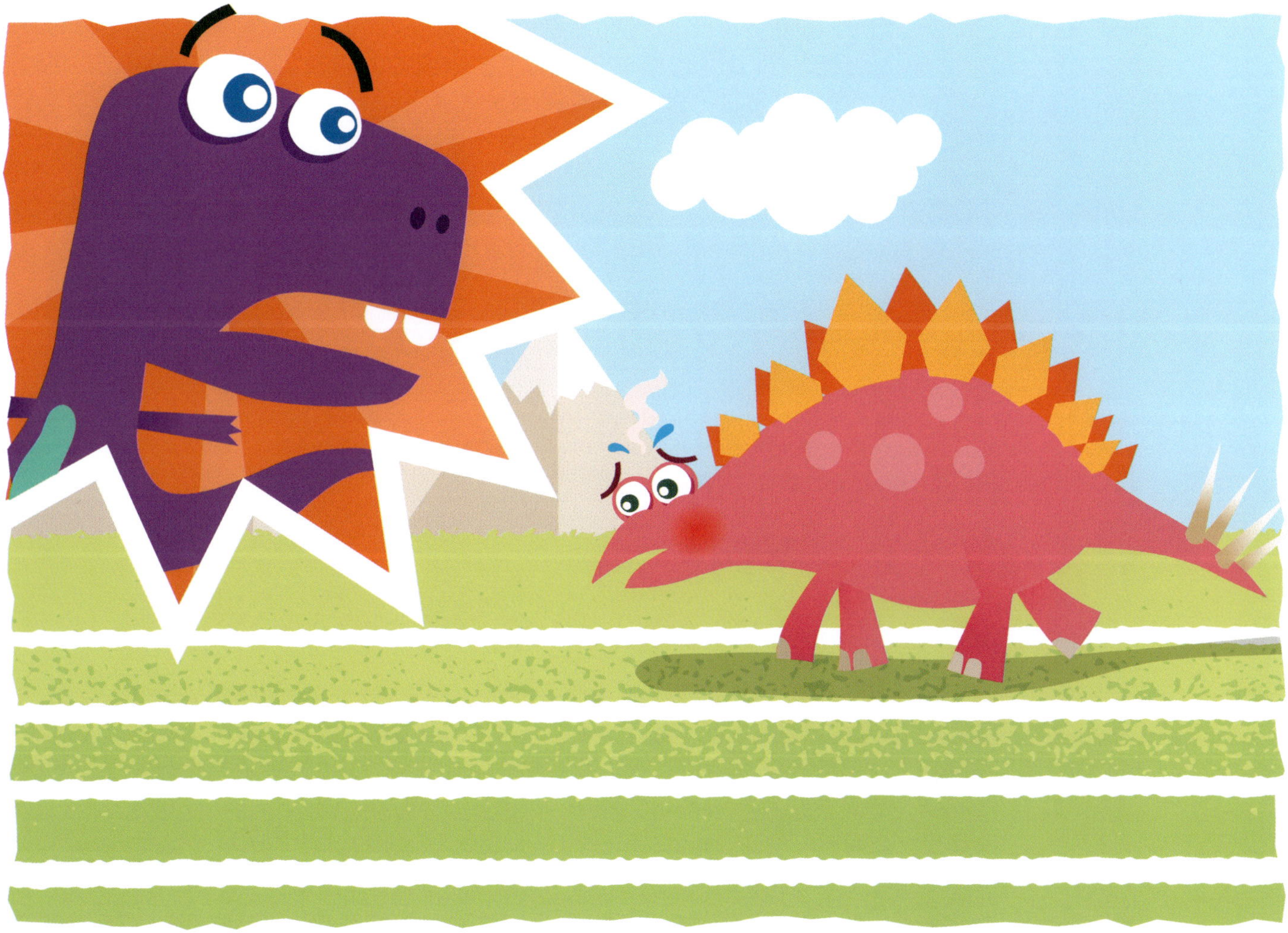

Archiesaurus wondered what to do, he wanted to be a good friend,

So he roared to everyone
"SLOW DOWN!"

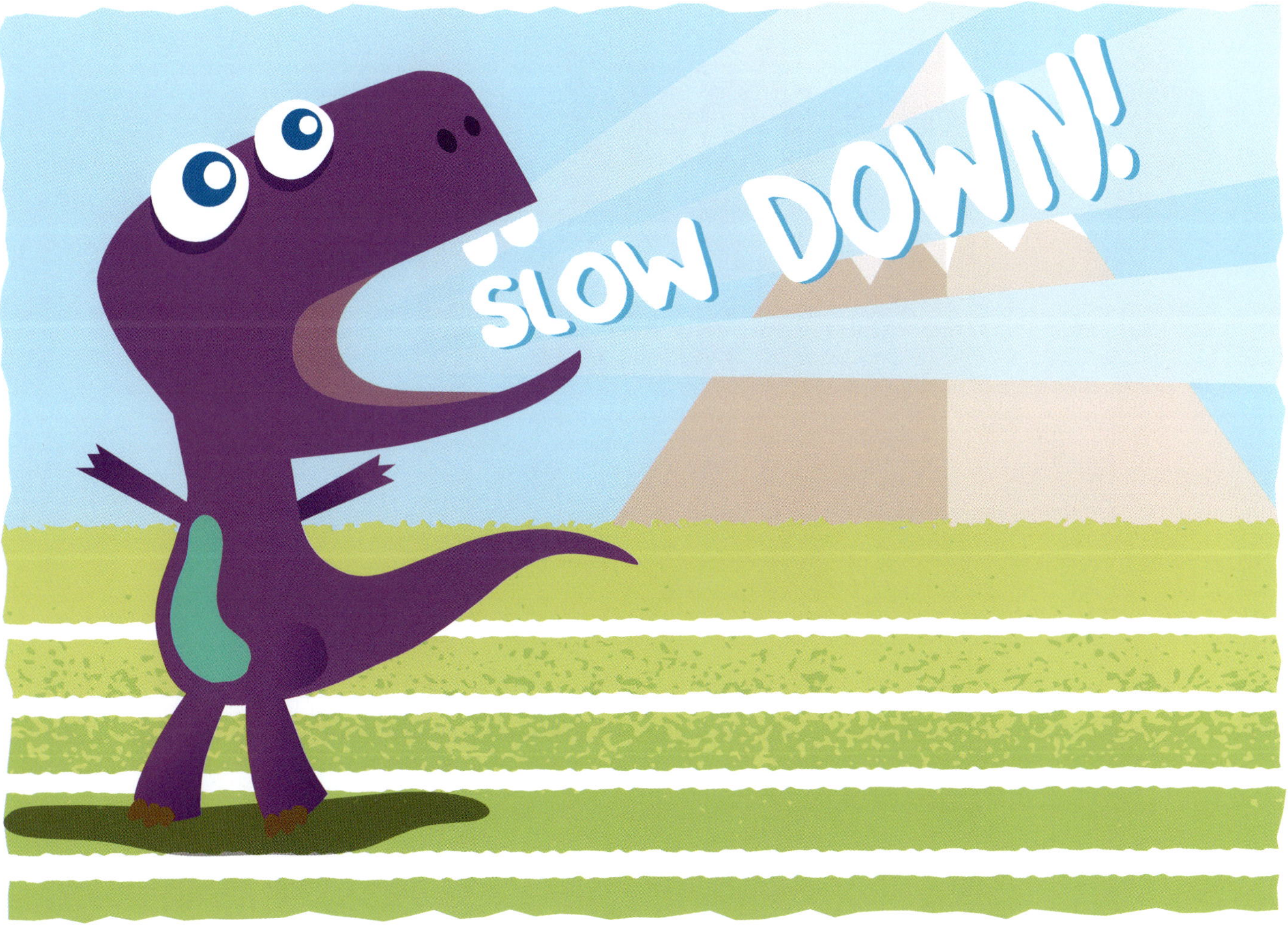
SLOW DOWN!

FINISH

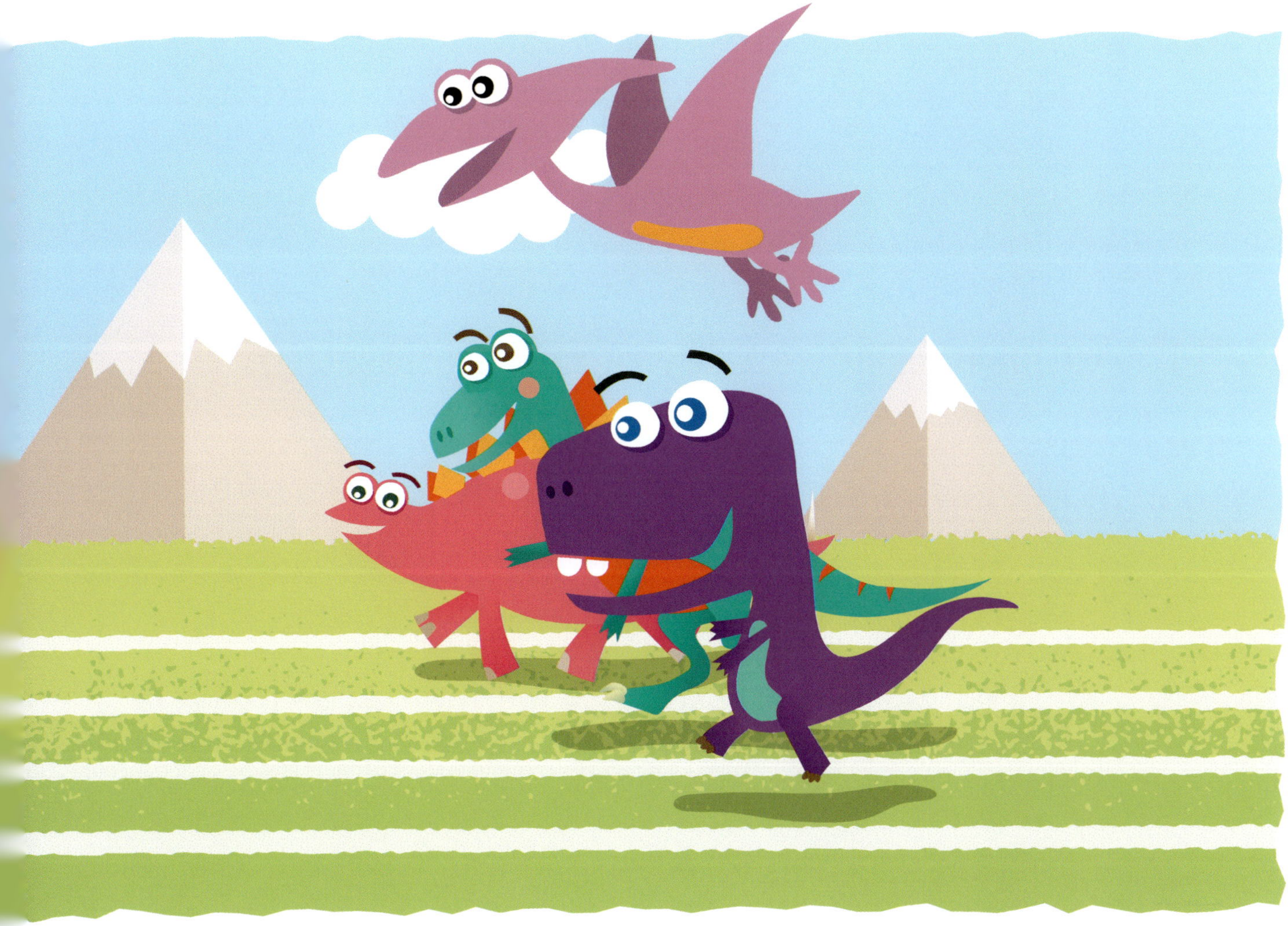

All the dinosaurs slowed down, and Steffosaurus caught up.
They all looked and laughed and together crossed the finishing line.

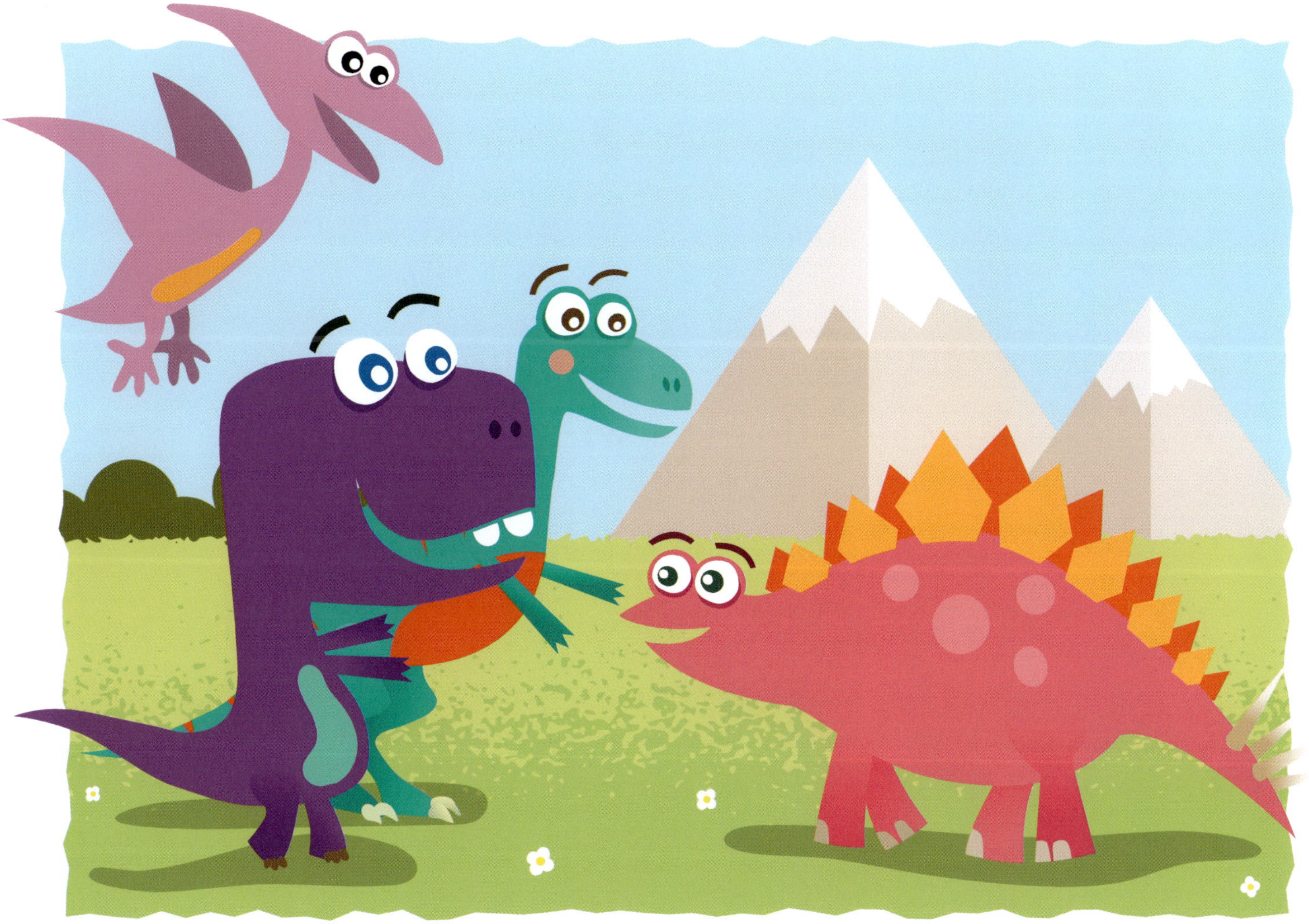

"**Thanks everyone**" said Steffosaurus happily, Archiesaurus said **"its ok, I will win next time!"**

THE END

Printed in Poland
by Amazon Fulfillment
Poland Sp. z o.o., Wrocław